THE CREATIVE CURRICULUM®
LearningGames®

Birth–12 Months

Joseph Sparling and Isabelle Lewis

Foreword by Diane Trister Dodge

Teaching Strategies Inc.
Washington, DC

This book of *LearningGames* is being shared with the family of

_____

Editor: Kai-leé Berke
Design: Carla Uriona
Layout/production: Tony MacFarlane and Abner Nieves

Published by:
Teaching Strategies, Inc.
P.O. Box 42243
Washington, DC 20015
www.TeachingStrategies.com

ISBN: 978-1-933021-58-4

Printed and bound in the United States of America

2012	2011	2010	2009	2008	2007
6	5	4	3	2	1

Contents

Foreword

Dear Parents,

It gives me great pleasure to introduce you to an exciting program called *The Creative Curriculum® LearningGames®*. The games are designed to build the kinds of skills that lead to successful, lifelong learning for your child. You are the key to making this happen.

On a regular basis you will be receiving a colorful handout describing simple and fun games to play with your child. They don't require any special toys or materials. You can do them as part of your everyday experiences with your child. But they can make a big difference, and they already have made a difference for thousands of children and families.

There are five different sets of *LearningGames* for children of different ages. You will receive only the games appropriate for your child. It's never too soon to start. Right from birth, your child is learning and growing. The experiences you provide during the first 5 years of life will help to build your child's brain, develop thinking skills, promote social skills, and build your child's confidence as a learner.

You are your child's first and most important teacher. Everything you do with your child, everything you say, every song you sing, and every object you give your child to play with teach important lessons. One of the wonderful results of using these games is that they help you to build a positive relationship with your child. And as your child is learning, you are as well. You will gain an understanding of child development and many practical ideas for guiding your child's learning.

Many programs using the *LearningGames* are also implementing either *The Creative Curriculum® for Infants, Toddlers & Twos* or *The Creative Curriculum® for Preschool*. As the lead author on these comprehensive curriculum materials, I am very excited to be able to offer this parent component, too. Children benefit the most when the important adults in their lives—their parents, caregivers, teachers, health care specialists, or home visitors—are working together to support their learning and growth.

I wish you great enjoyment and success,

Diane Trister Dodge
President
Teaching Strategies, Inc.

Acknowledgments

Many people helped in the preparation of *The Creative Curriculum* *LearningGames*. We would like to thank Kai-leé Berke and Heather Baker for their thoughtful writing contributions and for finding wonderful children's books that enhance each game. Thank you to Nancy Guadagno, Sharon Samber, Toni Bickart, and Rachel Tickner, our editors, for their attention to detail. We appreciate the work of Carla Uriona, who designed the new format for the activities, and Abner Nieves and Tony MacFarlane for their careful layout work. Thanks to Nancy Guadagno and Kai-leé Berke for their patience and persistence in moving the writing, editing, and production process forward.

THE CREATIVE CURRICULUM®
LearningGames®

Checklist for
The Creative Curriculum® LearningGames®:
Birth–12 months

I have shared the LearningGames *checked below with the family of* _____

Given to Family	LearningGames Activity Number and Title	Date Given to Family/Notes
☐	1. Building Trust	
☐	2. Songs and Rhythm Throughout the Day	
☐	3. Showing Your Baby Something Interesting	
☐	4. Soothing Your Baby	
☐	5. Talking to Your Baby	
☐	6. Holding and Dropping	
☐	7. Exploring a Face	
☐	8. Propping Up Your Baby	
☐	9. Peek-a-Boo	
☐	10. Searching for a Voice	
☐	11. Reach for It!	
☐	12. Watching a Toy Go Out of Sight	
☐	13. Rolling Over	
☐	14. Show Feelings	
☐	15. Turn and Find	
☐	16. Ride a Horsie	

Given to Family	LearningGames Activity Number and Title	Date Given to Family/Notes
☐	17. Sitting, Turning, and Reaching	
☐	18. Naming With a Mirror	
☐	19. Reading Pictures and Books	
☐	20. Making Da-Da-Da Sounds	
☐	21. Hiding and Finding	
☐	22. Introducing Strangers	
☐	23. Peek-a-Boo Mirror	
☐	24. Dropping Objects	
☐	25. Showing What Comes Next	
☐	26. Imitating Actions	
☐	27. Stand Up and Move	
☐	28. Puzzle Play	
☐	29. Hi and Bye-Bye	
☐	30. Providing Two Ways	
☐	31. First Crayons	
☐	32. Things to Taste	
☐	33. Find a Picture	
☐	34. Making Useful Choices	

What Your Child May Be Doing
Infants (Birth–12 Months)

Social/Emotional Development

Enjoy being held and cuddled

Respond to familiar people by smiling, cooing, and babbling (You are their favorite toy.)

Imitate people's actions

Explore toys by using their senses

Pay attention to sounds and movement

Enjoy playing peek-a-boo

Cognitive Development

Learn about objects by using all of their senses

Visually follow and respond to moving objects and faces

Like objects with contrasting colors and patterns and those with gentle movement and sounds

Watch their mirrored images appear and disappear

Imitate adult movements and language sounds

Enjoy activity boxes

Physical Development

Gain control of and move their heads from side to side

Play with hands and feet

Reach for, grasp, shake, mouth, and explore objects they can hold

Move objects from one hand to the other; bang objects together

Roll over

Sit on a blanket, propped at first and then without external support

Crawl to explore

Pull themselves to standing and cruise by holding on to furniture

Roll, hold, and throw balls

Pick up finger foods

Language and Literacy Development

Ask for care and attention by crying, laughing, and smiling, and through other vocalizations

Vocalize to themselves, other people, and toys

Understand and respond to gestures, facial expressions, and changes in vocal tone

Understand and respond to their names and to very simple, familiar requests

Take turns babbling, talking, and singing with others

Use gestures to communicate, such as pointing and head shaking

Enjoy listening to simple stories, rhymes, and songs

Use their senses to explore books

Building Trust

*I love you
so much.*

Communicate love through calm, warm body contact, and soothing words.

Responding to your baby in a loving way teaches her that she can trust you.

THE
CREATIVE CURRICULUM®
LearningGames®
Copyright 2007 Joseph Sparling

Why this is important

Your baby learns to love and trust from your loving words and actions. Responding to her in a positive way lets her know that she can trust you with her needs and feelings. When you hold her close while you feed her, the warmth of your body and the gentle sound of your voice help build her trust in you. When you respond to your baby's cries you are teaching her about communication. She is learning that her sounds cause something to happen that makes her feel comfortable again. Your baby's trust in one or two important people will give her the confidence and security she needs later to explore her world and build relationships with others.

What you do

- Go quickly to your baby when she expresses discomfort. This shows her that you care.

- Hold her close to you. Because she cannot yet understand your words, it is important to convey love with body language, facial expressions, and soothing sounds.

- Give her your full attention when taking care of her needs such as diapering, feeding, and bathing.

- Smile, cuddle, rock, and talk to her.

- Notice how your baby responds to you with sounds or movement. Let her know you understand she is communicating with you. *Oh, my sweet baby. I feel you snuggling into me. You are very sleepy.*

Another idea

Use this method of lovingly responding to her throughout the day. Your baby feels secure when you offer love consistently and confidently. If you feel like picking her up, do not wait until she cries. She will thrive on your attention and affection.

Let's read together!

Time for Bed
by Mem Fox

Songs and Rhythm Throughout the Day

Make your caregiving actions match the rhythm of a song.

By singing as you care for your baby, you help him learn to love music and feel comforted by soothing rhythm and motion.

Rub-a-dub-dub.

Why this is important

The crooning and stroking you do as you cradle your baby in your arms introduce him to music and rhythm. Your gentle touches and the sound of your voice offer much more to your baby than the sounds from a radio or TV. When you choose songs that have rhymes, you are getting your baby used to the patterns and sounds of words. This will help him later as he learns how to speak and then how to read.

What you do

- As you care for your baby, look for ways to use gentle, rhythmic motions and words. For example, when you rock your baby in a rocking chair, sing in time to the chair's motion. After feeding, you might pat his back while chanting, *Burp, burp, burp, here comes the burp.*

- Use calming words and rhythmic motions to soothe him when he cries. *Daddy loves you and Mommy does, too,* you sing over and over as you hold your baby and sway from side to side.

- Observe his body language as you move and sing. Does he appear content and relaxed in your arms? If not, try a different rhythmic motion.

Another idea

Extend this caregiving time a little beyond what is actually needed for the care—do it just for the pleasure it brings. Use songs and nursery rhymes to bring enjoyment to riding in the car, swinging in a baby swing, or going for walks in the stroller.

Let's read together!

Row, Row, Row Your Boat,
by Annie Kubler (illustrator)

Showing Your Baby Something Interesting

See the bunny?

Hold your baby or place him where he can hold his head up and look at interesting things.

This helps your baby learn to use his eyes and control his body.

Why this is important

Your baby will want to hold up his head and control his body movements in order to see something interesting such as your face or a colorful toy. The length of time he can hold his head up will get longer and longer. He will try harder when he is curious about an object. As his head control improves, so will his ability to use his body.

What you do

- Hold your baby to your shoulder. Keep your hand near, but let him support his own head as much as he can.

- Sit or stand so he sees something interesting over your shoulder such as another person, an animal, or light and shadows. If your baby is younger than 4 months old, hold him less than a foot away from the object.

- Talk to him and stroke him as he looks around in order to reinforce the positive experience.
  Do you see Grandma smiling at you?

Ready to move on?

Put him on a blanket indoors or outdoors so that he can observe you moving and working. Make sure that you can see and hear him. Stop often to smile and talk to him face-to-face.

Let's read together!

Smile!
by Roberta Grobel Intrater

Soothing Your Baby

Oh, my little baby. You're so sleepy.

Try different techniques to comfort your baby, such as holding, stroking, talking, and swaddling.

You learn what works best to soothe her, and she learns to trust that her needs will be met.

THE CREATIVE CURRICULUM® **LearningGames**®
Copyright 2007 Joseph Sparling

Why this is important

A newborn baby's actions are reflexive and her response to her world is very physical. When she feels content, her body is relaxed. When she feels distressed, she expresses it with her voice and through tension in her body. Your baby's trust in you grows each time you respond quickly to her needs. As you determine what calms your baby, you will begin to adjust your response to her needs and reactions. A baby who learns at an early age that her needs will be met cries less as she gets older. Learning to trust you will help her to have trust in herself and others.

What you do

- Pick up your baby and hold her to help her calm down when she shows distress.

- Respond to the tension in her body by swaddling her with a blanket and holding her close so that she can feel your warmth. To swaddle your baby, lay a blanket on a soft, flat surface. Position the blanket so that it looks like a diamond laid out in front of you. Fold down the top corner about six inches. Lay your baby on the blanket with the back of her neck on the top fold. Pull the corner on your right across your baby's shoulder and body, and tuck the edge under her back beneath her arm. Pull the bottom corner up over your baby's exposed shoulder, and tuck it under that shoulder. Bring the loose corner over your baby's exposed arm, across her body, and tuck it under her back. If your baby prefers to have her arms free, you can try swaddling her under her arms.

- Make eye contact, and speak softly to her: *My sweet baby, Mommy's here.* Continue to stroke and cuddle her as she calms down.

- Try making a rhythmic *shhh* sound or turn on a fan or static on the radio to imitate the *shhh* sound. In the first few months, many babies are soothed by a *shhh* sound which is similar to the sound they hear in their mother's womb.

Ready to move on?

As your baby gets older, try comforting her by using a gentle tone of voice and offering soothing touches before picking her up. If she does not calm down, pick her up and comfort her.

Let's read together!

Sleepytime Rhyme
by Remy Charlip

Talking to Your Baby

I hear you talking to me! Ahhhh.

Smile, hold your baby close so he can see your face and lips, and speak to him in a gentle voice.

Watching and listening to you speak helps your baby begin to connect the sound of a voice with mouth movement.

Why this is important

Back-and-forth vocal play helps your baby know that sounds and mouth movements usually go together. The pleasure of watching your face, combined with the sound of your voice, encourages him to practice making mouth noises. As your baby gets older, he will imitate the mouth movements he has seen and the sounds he has heard.

What you do

- Hold your baby close with his head cupped in your hands so that he can see your face and lips. Position him so that he is about 8 inches away from you. This is the distance that a young infant's eyes focus best on objects.

- Lean toward him and talk happily. Make sure he can see your lips move as he listens to the sounds: *I see your beautiful brown eyes. I feel your soft skin.*

- Pause to give your baby a chance to make sounds, though he may not try to make sounds right away. If he does not respond verbally, smile back at him and continue talking, pausing occasionally to give him time to respond.

- Smile and repeat back to him the sound he made when he makes any sound, accidentally or intentionally. This encourages him to continue making sounds.

Another idea

Try doing this back-and-forth vocal play during caregiving routines. Talk to your baby while you change his diaper, get him dressed, and give him a bath. Remember to pause to give him plenty of time to respond to your words. *Blue shirt ... Mommy is putting on your blue shirt.*

Let's read together!

Mommy Hugs
by Karen Katz

Holding and Dropping

Would you like to hold your rattle?

Offer toys that your baby can close her hand around.

This encourages her to use her hands to grasp and release objects.

Why this is important

When your baby learns to grasp, she begins a lifelong process of working with her hands. Hand skills such as buttoning a shirt, cutting with scissors, and writing with a pencil all begin with the ability to close her hand around an object. Young infants hold toys tightly because they have a gripping reflex. They do not yet know how to open their fingers. As your baby begins to move her fingers more purposefully, she will learn how to grasp the toy and intentionally release it. Dropping it shows she is making progress!

What you do

- Choose a toy that the baby can close her hand around easily, such as a soft animal or a rattle. Hold the toy so the baby can see it. **Remember to keep small objects out of her reach to avoid choking hazards.**

- Touch the toy to the inside of her hand so that her fingers close around it, as you describe it. Let go of the toy so that she can feel herself holding it. *This is your fuzzy lamb.*

- Repeat the game each time she drops the toy. *You dropped the fuzzy lamb. I will get it for you. Feel how soft the lamb is!*

- Encourage her to use each hand to hold the toy. *What about your other hand? Can you hold your rattle with this hand?*

Another idea

Vary the game by using objects with different textures. *Here is a bumpy rattle. Here is a smooth hippo.*

Let's read together!

My Fuzzy Farm Babies
by Tad Hills

Exploring a Face

Cheek. That's Momma's cheek.

Name the part of your face your baby touches the moment she touches it.

Allowing your baby to explore your face helps her begin to connect the word she hears with the part of the face she feels.

THE CREATIVE CURRICULUM® Learning Games®
Copyright 2007 Joseph Sparling

Why this is important

Very young infants have not yet learned that they can reach out and touch most things they see. As your baby grows, she will learn to move her hands purposefully toward an object. Your face is her most familiar object and frequently the one nearest to her. Allowing her to see and explore your facial features helps her gain better hand-eye coordination. Hearing words such as *eye*, *nose*, and *mouth* prepares her for identifying and naming her own body parts later when she starts talking.

What you do

- Encourage your baby to use her eyes and hands to explore your face. When she reaches for you, lean in closer so that she may comfortably touch you with her hands.

- Speak to her softly, naming each part and describing what she touches the moment she touches it. *You are touching Mommy's nose. Now you are touching Mommy's cheek.*

- Guide her to touch other parts of your face. For example, you might slowly turn your head to the side and guide her finger around the curves of your ear. *This is Mommy's ear.*

Another idea

As you do this activity with your baby, think of face movements that will seem surprising or funny to her such as blinking your eyelids, raising your eyebrows, wiggling your tongue, or puckering your lips. Smile and laugh with her.

Let's read together!

Baby Faces
by DK Publishing

Propping Up Your Baby

Use a pillow to prop up your baby so she can look around independently.

Propping her up allows your baby to explore more easily with her eyes and hands.

Who's in that mirror?

THE
CREATIVE CURRICULUM®
Learning Games®
Copyright 2007 Joseph Sparling

Why this is important

Propping your baby up on a pillow allows her to hold her head up and look at objects and the people around her. When your baby is flat on her stomach or back, her exploration is limited. She may see only the rug under her or the ceiling above her. With her chest elevated or when you prop her in a sitting position she can observe what is going on around her and use her hands to explore toys placed directly in front of her. As your baby spends time in these positions, her muscle control will increase and she will be able to bend and reach for objects.

What to do

Place a pillow under your baby so that her tummy rests on it and her arms are out in front of her. This position allows her to hold up her head and look around. Observe your baby carefully and help her if she slips. On the pillow she may push with her legs or roll sideways. **Do not leave your baby unattended during this activity.**

- Place a few toys near her hands so that she can see and touch them. Try holding a mirror in front of her. Notice how she watches the baby in the mirror.

- Talk about the objects as she explores each one. *You're looking at the yellow bunny rattle.*

- If she prefers sitting up, place firm pillows behind her back so that she is sitting, leaning back, with her head supported comfortably. Position the pillows to prevent her from falling over. Place a few soft pillows in front of her in case she falls forward.

- Place objects in different positions around her to encourage her to practice moving her head to look at something to explore.

Let's read together!

Bright Baby Animals
by Roger Priddy

Another idea

Prop your baby in a seated position on the floor in a room where you are working. Talk to her as you work. For example, as you fold laundry, lay a blanket on the floor and prop her up with firm pillows, making sure she is securely supported on all sides. Explain to her what you are doing and stop frequently to touch her gently while including her in your work. *I'm folding the blue towel. Feel how soft that is against your cheek.*

Peek-a-Boo

Where's my baby?

With your baby facing you, talk to her from behind a cloth, and then peek out.

Over time, your baby will learn that you are still there even when she cannot see you.

Why this is important

An infant cannot understand the permanence of objects. When an item is gone from her sight, she thinks it has disappeared. Talking to her from behind the cloth helps her to learn that your face is there even though it is covered. Over time your child will learn that a toy or face still exists even though she may not see it. This concept is essential to her security as she begins to crawl and walk out of sight of familiar people.

What you do

- Cover your face with a light towel or baby blanket while facing your baby. Talk to her from behind the cover, and then whisk it away or peek around the cloth while saying, *Peek-a-boo!*

- Alternate between covering your face and hers. Each time, be sure to talk to her through each step of the game: *I'm looking for my baby. Where is the baby?*

- Look for signs that she is trying to remove the blanket herself. She may thrash her arms and legs or rub the blanket with her fists. Help her if she cannot grasp the blanket and pull it off.

- After playing the game over a period of time, gradually take longer to pull the blanket away. If she successfully pulls the blanket, show surprise and excitement at seeing her again: *You found Momma! I'm so happy to see you!*

- Remove the blanket quickly if she appears distressed by the game. Make sure that during the game she can always see part of you so that she feels secure.

Another idea

Play the game during routine times of day. Anything can be used to hide behind—a shirt, washcloth, diaper, or bib.

Let's read together!

Peek-a-Boo!
by Roberta Grobel Intrater

Searching for a Voice

Hi, James! I'm all the way over here!

Call your baby's name from a distance so he can practice locating your voice.

This helps him learn how to locate the source of a sound.

THE CREATIVE CURRICULUM® LearningGames®
Copyright 2007 Joseph Sparling

Why this is important

Locating sounds that are out of sight encourages your baby to use his eyes and ears to identify the sound and to use muscle control to turn his head in your direction. When he is older, these skills will help him pay attention to a voice from another room, recorded music, or signals for safety.

What you do

- Place your baby on his back and move to a position a few feet away. Speak his name softly several times until he attempts to turn toward the sound: *James, can you see me? I'm over here.*

- Allow time for him to try to find you. He may not turn his head until he realizes he cannot see you in front of him.

- Smile, pick him up, and cuddle him when he successfully turns to look at you. If he cannot find you, move closer to him while you continue talking until he sees you.

- Move to another position in the room and repeat the game until your baby loses interest or becomes fussy.

Ready to move on?

When your baby is comfortable lying on his stomach, try the game from that position. While on his stomach he must manage the weight of his head as well as the direction, so he may not look at you as quickly or for as long.

Let's read together!

Big Baby Book
by Helen Oxenbury

Reach for It!

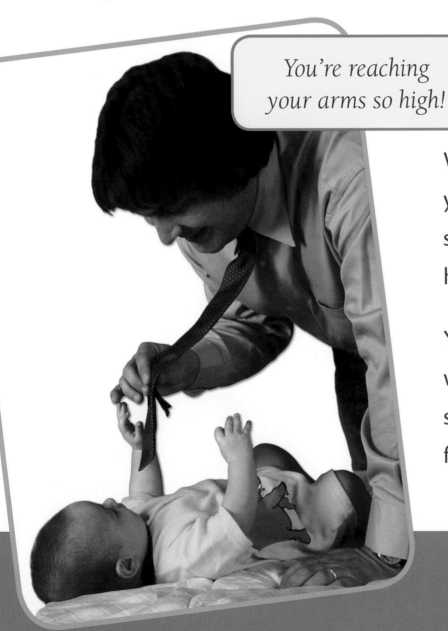

You're reaching your arms so high!

When your baby reaches for your tie or scarf, use your smile and voice to tell him he did something special.

Your baby learns that you will give him your biggest smile each time he reaches for your tie.

THE
CREATIVE CURRICULUM®
LearningGames®
Copyright 2007 Joseph Sparling

Why this is important

Your baby will need to know how to make his hands and eyes work together in order to reach objects. At first he will only kick and swat randomly. When he gains better control of his hands, he will grab an object and play with it. The good feeling he gets from your positive reaction to his efforts encourages him to practice this skill and increases his understanding of cause and effect.

What you do

- Tie a scarf or necktie around your neck so the ends dangle in front of your baby.

- Shake the scarf or tie gently to draw his attention to it, or help him by first touching the material to his hand.

- Smile broadly and talk to him when he makes any move toward the scarf or tie. This encourages him to reach again. *You grabbed Daddy's tie. You are so strong.* **Do not leave your baby unattended with a scarf, tie, or other material such as beads, string, or cords longer than 6 inches. These are strangulation hazards. Also avoid choking hazards by making sure that beads, bells, etc. cannot come loose and be swallowed.**

Another idea

In order to encourage your baby to continue playing the game, vary the objects you hang around your neck. He may enjoy reaching for a beaded string, a soft toy, or a bell. Introduce a variety of textures and colors by altering the item each time.

Let's read together!

Pat the Bunny
by Dorothy Kunhardt

Watching a Toy Go Out of Sight

Move a toy out of sight, make a noise with it, and then return it.

Seeing a toy disappear and always immediately return helps your baby begin learning that things are still there when they are out of sight.

Jingle, jingle…

Where did it go?

THE CREATIVE CURRICULUM® LearningGames®

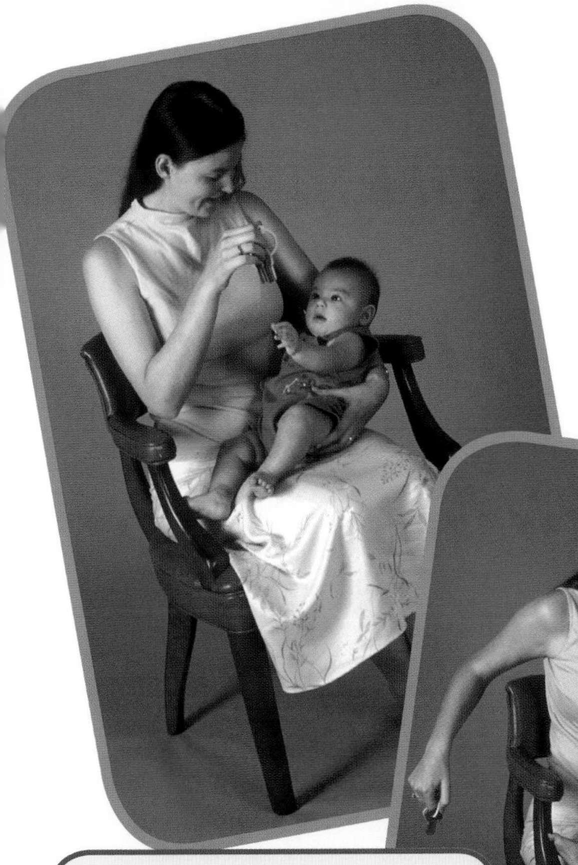

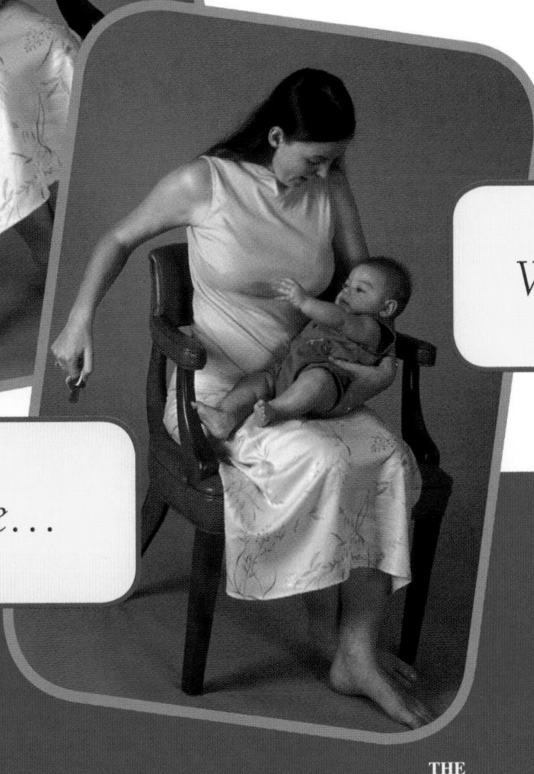

Why this is important

Babies begin following moving objects with their eyes almost as soon as they are born. They continue to develop this skill as they grow. When you move a toy out of your baby's sight she may lose interest and look away. However, she may continue to look for it if she hears a rattling or jingling sound from the out-of-sight object. She will eventually learn that when people or things go out of sight, they are not necessarily gone forever.

What you do

- Support your baby on your lap so that you can see her eyes. Hold a toy where her eyes are looking.

- Move the toy slowly and notice the way she follows it with her eyes. After a few moments, give her the toy to play with while offering kisses and encouraging words. *You watched Mommy move your keys back and forth and up and down.*

- Keep the game interesting by changing the direction of the moving object and by using different toys.

- Choose a noisy toy and move it out of her sight after she has had success following a toy with her eyes.

- Observe how she reacts when she can no longer see or hear the toy. Make a noise with the hidden toy and then bring it out for her to see and play with.

Ready to move on?

Think of creative ways to make the toy disappear and reappear. The toy can hide under a blanket or shirt, peek behind a curtain, or sit under a hat.

Let's read together!

Playtime Peekaboo
by DK Publishing

Rolling Over

Move a toy so that your baby will try to turn his body in order to keep the toy in sight.

Offering the child a toy in this way gives him a reason to try to roll over.

You're rolling over to get the toy!

THE
CREATIVE CURRICULUM®
Learning Games®
Copyright 2007 Joseph Sparling

Why this is important

Your baby needs to know how to turn over so that he can crawl, change position, and make himself comfortable. At first he may only follow an object with his eyes when you move it in front of his face. Later, as you move the toy, he may turn his head and try to roll his body to keep the toy in sight. Rolling from a smooth surface onto a textured one will help him realize that he has moved his body to a new place. Awareness of his body will help him move purposefully later as he begins to crawl and walk.

What you do

- Lay your baby on his back on a smooth surface. Put a fuzzy or textured blanket next to him.

- Sit behind his head and hold a favorite toy or a noise-making toy above him so that he can see it comfortably.

- Move the toy slowly in different directions, side to side, while making sure his eyes follow the toy.

- Move the toy far to the side and toward the top of his head, as you talk about what he sees. *Your elephant is moving over here. Can you hear it rattle?* Notice your baby follow the toy with his eyes.

- If your baby reaches by arching his back and turning his head, encourage him with words, but do not help him roll over. *You almost have it. You are really stretching!*

- Give him the toy when he turns over. *You rolled over to reach your elephant!* Talk with him about the textured blanket he is now lying on. *You rolled onto a fuzzy blanket.* If he keeps trying but cannot completely roll over, slightly nudge his lower body to help.

Ready to move on?

When your baby can roll over easily, show him the toy and then place it next to him on the blanket where he will find it when he rolls.

Let's read together!

Red, Blue, Yellow Shoe
by Tana Hoban

Show Feelings

Up, up you go!

Smile and laugh to show your feelings as you raise your baby and say *up* or lower your baby and say *down.*

Expressing your happiness encourages your baby to join in the expression, too.

Down you come!

THE
CREATIVE CURRICULUM®
LearningGames®
Copyright 2007 Joseph Sparling

Why this is important

When you express your excitement and happiness your baby will be encouraged to join in and show these same feelings. Expressing several basic emotions is not difficult for an infant, but she needs the adults around her to help her learn which emotions are appropriate at different times. When you show a joyful approach to games and learning, your child is likely to be cheerful, too. This activity also encourages her language development.

What you do

- Hold your baby around her chest and under her arms. Smile at her.

- Raise her over your head gently and slowly saying, *Up* or *Up you go*. Lower her saying, *Down* or *Down you come*. Then hug her close to your body.

- Maintain eye contact with your baby as you lift her up and down to help her feel connected to you.

- Smile, laugh, and talk so she can tell by your face and words that you have happy feelings about the game and that her feeling of excitement is appropriate. If this is new to your child, she may look a little worried or gasp when she's lifted high in the air. When she sees you smiling, she will begin to feel good about the movement.

- Go slowly so you don't startle her with movements that are too fast. Give her time to smile and respond to you with cooing or babbling.

Another idea

You can do this activity during routine times of the day such as when you lift her in and out of her crib or onto the changing table, or put her down to play on a blanket.

Let's read together!

Baby Faces
by Margaret Miller

Turn and Find

You turned around and found it!

Turn your baby so she will need to look behind her body to see a toy.

Changing your baby's position so that a toy is out of sight encourages her to remember the toy and move her body to find it.

Why this is important

Showing your baby a toy and then moving her so she cannot see it encourages her to remember it and move her body to find it. Memory, like her other skills, develops in stages. Turning her head or body to regain sight of an object shows the beginning development of a type of memory called object permanence.

What you do

- Sit at a table with your baby in your lap. Show her a favorite toy and place it on the table while talking about the toy. *See the baby bear! What a friendly bear!*

- Turn your baby so that she faces away from the object. If she tries to turn her head or body to see the toy, encourage her to look and find it.

- Give her the toy. Smile and speak lovingly to her. *You turned around and found the bear!*

- Notice her interest in the game. If she does not look for the toy, try again at a later time.

Another idea

Lay your child on the floor on her stomach with the toy in front of her. Slide her quickly around so the toy is at her side (from a twelve o'clock to a three o'clock position). She may wiggle back to the original position or roll onto her back to look for the toy. Allow her time to find the toy herself before offering help.

Let's read together!

Ready, Set, Go!
by Nina Laden

Ride a Horsie

Ride a horsie up and down!

Do a special action on the same one or two words in a rhyme and see if your baby notices.

Your baby will learn to look forward to certain words and their matching actions.

Why this is important

Babies enjoy all kinds of rhythm games. By moving your baby in a special way when you say a certain word in a song, your baby will learn to look forward to the particular word that signals the special event. This helps your baby learn that words can tell her what is happening to her. Hearing a rhyme repeated and moving to it in the same fun way gives her confidence in her ability to predict what will happen next.

What you do

- Hold your baby on your lap as you say the rhyme: *Ride-a-horsie, ride-a-horsie, ride him into town. Ride-a-horsie, ride-a-horsie, up and down.* Gently bounce her to the rhythm of the rhyme.

- Bounce your baby high when you say *up*; when you say *down*, bounce her low.

- Make eye contact with your baby so that she can see your smiling face and you can see what she is feeling during the game.

- Repeat the rhyme and movements several times, then try pausing before saying *up* and *down*. She may show you she knows what will happen next by laughing, kicking her feet, or trying to move her body high and low.

Another idea

Try the game using other songs and rhymes such as "This Is the Way the Farmer Rides," which uses changing rhythms and motions. Choose a special word or words and move your baby in a different way when you sing those words in the song.

Let's read together!

Up!
by Kristine O'Connell George

Sitting, Turning, and Reaching

You're reaching high!

Hold toys in various positions to encourage your baby to stretch and reach for the toys.

Your baby will practice using his hands and body to reach objects and will gain better balance for sitting.

You're reaching to the side!

Why this is important

Providing an interesting object for your baby to reach encourages him to stretch and balance himself while also learning to sit alone. Once he can comfortably sit alone, he will not need his hands for support. Instead, he can use his hands to explore his surroundings. Seeing objects out of reach will eventually inspire him to try new ways to get them, such as crawling.

What you do

- Begin the game with your baby sitting securely on your lap with your arm wrapped around his waist.

- Hold a noise-making or favorite toy in front of him—just far enough that he needs to lean forward slightly and stretch his arms to reach it. *Can you reach the rattle? Look how you can stretch!*

- Offer encouraging words and hugs when he reaches the toy, while allowing him to play with the object.

- Repeat the game, moving the toy to a new location just within his reach. Be sure to support his body as needed.

- Try moving the toy to his side and observe how he tries to reach it. Does he move his arms and trunk? Does he try to use only one arm? Encourage him to move in a variety of ways by moving the toy to different positions around his body.

Ready to move on?

Try the game with the baby seated on the floor. If necessary, place pillows around him for support. Let him practice reaching in different directions for the toy by placing it in a variety of locations just within his reach.

Let's read together!

Baby Love
by Sandra Magsamen

Naming With a Mirror

Cheek! I'm touching your cheek.

Touch and name parts of your baby's face as she looks in the mirror.

Your baby will gradually begin to recognize herself and her body parts as you point them out to her.

Where's your nose?

Why this is important

Feeling the touch of your finger on her mouth at the same time that she sees it happen in the mirror gives her a better understanding of the word *mouth*. At first your child will not understand that she is the baby in the mirror. Over time as you play this game with your baby, she will begin to understand that the mirror shows her image. With your help she will learn to recognize the names of body parts. Learning about herself helps her develop a positive sense of self.

What you do

- Sit with your baby or stand holding her in front of a mirror. Talk to your baby while she looks at her reflection. *See the baby? See Annie in the mirror?*

- If your child has not had many experiences with the mirror, she may be surprised to see you in two places. Acknowledge the new experience. *Yes, Mommy is holding you and you see Mommy in the mirror.*

- Touch your child's mouth and say, *Mouth*.

- Try the game with different body parts, especially parts of her face, to help her recognize each one.

Ready to move on?

After many days of this game, alter it by no longer touching her mouth as you speak. Say the word *mouth* or ask, *Where is your mouth?* Allow your baby time to find her mouth. If she does not find it or does not try to find it, gently guide her hand to her mouth.

Let's read together!

Pretty Brown Face
by Andrea & Brian Pinkney

Reading Pictures and Books

Banana. Yum!

Notice what your baby is looking at in a book and name that picture.

When you name the picture at the moment he is showing interest in it, he will begin to understand more of your words.

Why this is important

Seeing the pictures and hearing the names of objects on the page help your baby to connect pictures and words. When you place an object next to its picture, you deepen your child's understanding that pictures represent real things. A positive introduction to pictures and books is an important step in your child's literacy development.

What you do

- Collect cards or board books with one simple picture on each page.

- Show a card or picture book to your child and name the object on the page at the moment he looks at it.

- Tell him in simple words about its color, shape, or use: *This is a shoe. A red shoe. You wear it on your foot.*

- Give him the picture to hold and explore, and continue to talk to him about the picture.

Another idea

Pair a picture with an object the baby is familiar with. For example, if you have a picture of a cat, invite him to hold his toy cat as you show him the picture. Talk to him about the object in the picture and the object in your hand: *That's a cat. The cat is furry. You have a toy cat.* Acknowledge his attempts to talk about the picture. *I hear you talking about that cat.*

Let's read together!

Good Morning, Sun
by Lisa Campbell Ernst

Making Da-Da-Da Sounds

Imitate sounds that your baby makes, especially repeated sounds like *da-da-da* or *ma-ma*.

Soon, some of these repeated sounds may turn into your baby's very first words: *mama*, *dada*, or *bye-bye*.

Da-da-da-da.

Da-da-da!

THE CREATIVE CURRICULUM®
LearningGames®

Why this is important

When your baby begins to make sounds, both purposely and accidentally, you can encourage her to repeat those sounds. After practicing a sound, she will later be able to recall the sound and distinguish it from others. Repeating sounds develops the skill that will enable her to eventually repeat words. Oral language development (learning to talk and understand the words they hear) is an important part of early literacy development for young children.

What you do

- Hold your baby so she can see your face.

- Repeat a sound back to her that you have heard her make. Move your lips distinctly and make the sound clear: *Da-da-da*.

- Observe her watching your mouth move. She may move her lips and tongue as she attempts to use her voice. Wait for her to make the sound again.

- Encourage her by giving her plenty of time to respond and by repeating the sound.

- Acknowledge her attempts to make the sound back to you. *You're talking!* Take turns with your baby in saying the sound.

Another idea

Try the many different sounds you've heard your baby make, such as *da, ma, bi, bu,* and *me*. Be sure to focus on one sound at a time. Making the sound into a song by changing your voice pitch or the tempo of the syllables keeps your baby interested longer.

Let's read together!

Baby Says
by John Steptoe

Hiding and Finding

Can you find the toy?

Invite your baby to look for an object that she watches you hide.

Because she sees you hide the object, over time she will understand that objects that are hidden can be found.

THE
CREATIVE CURRICULUM®
LearningGames®
Copyright 2007 Joseph Sparling

Why this is important

By hiding something while your baby watches, you help her understand that objects she no longer sees can still exist. This understanding is called object permanence. It will give her confidence and security to know that people and things exist even when they are out of her sight.

What you do

- Show your baby a special toy.

- Talk about the toy and let her explore it while you keep it in your hand.

- Hide the toy behind your back or in your pocket making sure she watches. Ask about the toy. *Where did the doggie go? Where is it? Can you see it?* If she does not look for the toy or looks only at the place where the toy was, show it to her again before partially hiding it from view.

- Offer positive feedback when she finds it and bring it out for her to hold. *You found the dog! He was hiding behind Mommy's back!*

- Repeat the game by hiding the toy in a new place.

Another idea

Find other times to play this game. As you care for her throughout the day, hide something briefly for her to find. *Where is your shoe? Can you find it?*

Let's read together!

Where's Nicky?
by Cathryn Falwell

Introducing Strangers

Here's something for you!

Help your baby meet new people by having them stand back and approach your baby gently, sometimes holding out a familiar toy.

Slowly introducing your baby to strangers may help him feel comfortable when meeting new people.

Why this is important

Your child is curious about new people and objects in his environment. However, he has probably begun to express a preference for a few special adults. Most babies between 6 and 12 months may be uncomfortable with visitors, even close relatives. Often he will prefer to get to know a new person from the comfort and safety of your arms. By being supportive during these meetings, you build his confidence and comfort around others.

What you do

- Hold your baby securely when introducing him to a new person. Use your own friendly gestures and words to make your child feel comfortable. Shake hands with the stranger: *Hello. It's so nice to see you!*

- Help him touch the newcomer's hand for a moment, if your baby seems willing.

- Invite the visitor to hand your baby a familiar toy or an attractive object. Ask the visitor to stand back a little. If your child reaches out for the toy, he is making a choice to interact with the new person.

- Encourage your baby to show a favorite toy to the visitor, by handing it to your child. *Do you want to show Aunt Laura your bunny rabbit?*

Ready to move on?

When your baby is ready to go to a new adult, stay close so he can see you but do not try to maintain eye contact with your child. If you appear busy with something nearby your child will know you are close but he can focus his attention on the new person instead of on you. His first physical contact with a new person may last only a few seconds. Be ready to hold him again when he indicates he wants you.

Let's read together!

Is Your Mama a Llama?
by Deborah Guarino

Peek-a-Boo Mirror

Peek-a-boo!

Encourage your baby to remove a cloth from a mirror to see what is there.

Your baby will discover that he can make things happen, like causing his own reflection to appear.

Look at you!

Why this is important

Encouraging your baby to play in front of a mirror helps him practice finding his reflection. When you first pull the cloth away from the mirror, your baby may be surprised to see his image. At first he may touch the image and talk to the baby in the mirror, not recognizing his reflection. Over time he will begin to understand that he is the baby in the mirror. This helps him establish an understanding of himself.

What you do

- Attach a cloth to the top of a sturdy, unbreakable mirror. Hold your baby on your lap in front of the uncovered mirror.

- Point to the image and talk about the baby: *See the baby? That's you, Juan. Look at your smile!*

- Cover the mirror as you ask, *Where is Juan?* Wait to see what he will do. If he lifts the cloth or pulls at it, respond positively. *Peek-a-boo! You moved the cloth; look at you!* If he needs help, lift the cloth a little so he can see part of his face. Show surprise and pleasure as he sees himself. *I see something under there. It's you, Juan!*

Another idea

Sit with your baby on the floor with the unbreakable mirror in front of him. Play the game with him a few times before moving back and encouraging him to play by himself. Let him see you in the background through the mirror.

Let's read together!

The Big Book of Beautiful Babies
by David Ellwand

Dropping Objects

See the block fall?

Invite your baby to practice dropping things, especially things that make a noise when they land.

Picking up and dropping objects helps your baby gain more control of the muscles in her hands.

Why this is important

At this age, your baby can hold things very well but cannot always let them go when she wants. Opening her fingers is a different process from closing them, and learning to control the muscles in her hands will take her a lot of time and practice. Early hand control helps her manipulate objects during play. Later, she will need to control the muscles in her hands when she starts holding crayons and pencils for drawing.

What you do

- Show her a toy in your hand. When she looks at it, open your fingers and let the toy drop.

- Repeat the motion, saying *Drop* as it falls. Keep a short dropping distance so she'll be able to see your hand and the dropped object at the same time.

- Encourage her to try after you have shown her several times.

- Give an enthusiastic response with each attempt she makes. *Wow! You dropped the block by yourself!*

- Play again using a ball that bounces or a bell that makes a noise when it hits the floor. She may show more interest in a toy that produces a sound when dropped.

- Listen for any sounds she makes when she lets go of the ball. This is her attempt to imitate you when you say, *Drop.*

Another idea

Try playing the game during bath time. Dropping objects in the water makes a fun splash that may encourage her to continue practicing her new skill.

Let's read together!

Dear Zoo
by Rod Campbell

Showing What Comes Next

Keys. We're going to get in the car now.

Show your baby a familiar object and tell him what you are going to do with it.

Doing this makes it possible for your baby to think ahead to the next event.

Why this is important

Your baby will begin to understand what comes next when you first show him a related familiar object. As he associates objects with actions and words, he begins to make sense of his world. The social experience of showing someone something is good preparation for the time later when he will share and take turns with another person.

What you do

- Call to your baby from across the room.

- Show him an object related to what is going to happen next. The object could be a toy, a blanket, a bottle, or a diaper.

- Give him a chance to locate you in the room and turn toward you.

- Hold up the object again, name it, and talk about what is going to happen next. *Here is your bottle. Would you like me to feed you?*

- Try the game when dressing him or bathing him. *I have your lotion. It's time for your night-night massage.* Give him a moment to anticipate the next step before you do it.

Another idea

Expand the game beyond caretaking activities. Show him the vase before you pour water and place flowers into it, or show him a wind-up toy before you wind it up and make it go.

Let's read together!

Ten, Nine, Eight
by Molly Bang

Imitating Actions

You're banging on the pan!

Bang, bang!

Do some actions that your baby can copy.

This helps him use an important type of learning: imitation.

Why this is important

You can take advantage of your baby's natural interest in what you do and encourage him to copy your actions. Providing many opportunities for your child to copy your actions helps him begin to use imitation as a way of learning. Many actions, such as talking, eating with a fork, or driving a car, depend—in some way—on good imitation.

What you do

- Sit down with your child. Hold a spoon and pan, and offer your baby a spoon to hold. Hit the pan with the spoon while saying *Bang, bang, bang!*

- Invite your baby to hit the pan, too. He may bang the pan right away, or he might spend more time watching you before he tries it.

- Offer positive feedback when he tries to bang with the spoon, even if his movements are incomplete. *You did what I did! You're banging with the spoon!*

- Repeat the game with other motions such as tapping the pan with your hands, or using a different object instead of a spoon. Keep the movements simple, and use slow, exaggerated motions that he can follow.

- Try copying your baby when he makes a movement different than yours.

Another idea

Try the game using songs and rhymes with hand motions such as "Pat-a-cake." You can clap your hands once while saying *clap*. You may also try spreading your arms wide and saying *big*. Think of other simple gestures your baby may want to imitate.

Let's read together!

Little Mister
by Randy Duburke

Stand Up and Move

You're moving on your own!

Arrange furniture so your baby can pull up to a standing position and try taking a few steps while holding on.

Your baby will have the chance to practice with confidence when you give her objects to help her stand and take steps.

THE CREATIVE CURRICULUM®
LearningGames®

Why this is important

Moving while standing up and holding on to something comes before walking independently. Your baby first must learn to support her own weight and find her balance as she practices standing. As she takes sideways steps while holding on to furniture, she will feel excited and will want to try walking independently.

What you do

- Once your baby can pull herself to a standing position, place a few chairs in a row, and put a toy on the first chair with your child standing in front of it.

- Put a second toy on the next chair after she plays with the first toy. Stand back and see if she will move from chair to chair.

- Do not make her stand again if she sits to play with the toy. Let her move at her own pace.

- Gradually move the chairs slightly apart as she gets better at the game.

- Pick her up and cuddle her when she finishes. Let her know you are happy for her accomplishment.

Let's read together!

I Love You Through and Through
by Bernadette Rossetti Shustak

Ready to move on?

Let your baby move independently for a few steps with the support of a cardboard box. Stand your child beside the box and offer support while placing her hands on one edge for balance. Keep your hand on the box to steady it. She may move it accidentally at first as she shuffles her feet to maintain her balance. Offer encouragement for her new skill. *You're using the box to help you walk!*

Puzzle Play

Can you put the ball in the hole?

You can invent a first puzzle for your baby by letting him put items in a muffin pan.

A simple coordination game gives your baby the opportunity to practice fitting objects together.

Why this is important

By placing items in a muffin pan, your baby gains skill in judging sizes and shapes with his eyes and testing them with his hands. He will enjoy holding the ball and fitting it into the pan. Each time he practices picking up the items in this simple puzzle and moving them, he learns more coordination.

What you do

- Look for objects around the house that will fit into the cup of a muffin pan. The fit needs to be fairly snug so it feels like a puzzle. Apples, oranges, and balls work well.

- Sit with your child and encourage him to explore the pieces in front of him. *You're putting the apple in the hole!*

- Follow his cues to determine his interest level. Allow him to use the pieces in other ways. *You took the ball out of the pan and now you're rolling it on the floor.*

- Try counting the pieces, talking about colors and textures, and describing your child's actions.

Another idea

Look for other opportunities in your day to offer your baby a simple puzzle game. For example, he may enjoy putting a rubber stopper in the sink or fitting the telephone in its cradle.

Let's read together!

Funny Fingers Circus
by Karin Blume

Hi and Bye-Bye

Bye-bye!

Say *Hi* and *Bye-bye* (or *Good-bye*) to your baby, the same way you greet others.

Using standard greetings with your baby helps her learn to wave and say *Hi* and *Bye-bye,* too.

Why this is important

By waving and saying *Hi* and *Bye-bye* to your baby at appropriate times, you provide a model of conversational behavior. By responding joyfully to her attempts to communicate *Hi* and *Bye-bye*, you encourage her to try to repeat those actions. Because the gesture of waving is widely understood, it provides her with an opportunity to communicate with people outside of her immediate family.

What you do

- Smile and say *Hi* when you approach your baby or when she makes an *ah* sound (this may be her attempt at saying *Hi*). Wave to her to get her attention.

- Use greetings during daily routines, such as diaper changing, mealtime, and bath time. For example, when you baby makes the *ah* sound during a diaper change, pause, move closer to her face, smile, and say *Hi* in a gentle voice.

- Observe your baby. She will listen and watch you. She may smile back and then, over time, begin to imitate the sound and motion. Look for signs such as her fingers moving slightly in her lap. She will likely use the hand motion or the sound of *Hi* separately before putting the two together.

- Wave and say *Bye-bye* or *Good-bye* when leaving a room.

- Encourage others to greet her the same way, and help her wave her hand or wiggle her fingers to participate in this early form of conversation.

Another idea

You can help your baby practice greeting others throughout the day. Stand at the door and wave to people walking outside. Greet the cashier at the grocery store or the nurse in the doctor's office and encourage your child to do the same.

Let's read together!

Baby Says Bye-Bye
by Opal Dunn

Providing Two Ways

Can you drop it in?

You found it!

Use a box with two holes to let your baby discover how to retrieve a toy that has gone out of reach.

Finding two ways to reach the toy gives her practice in solving problems with more than one solution.

Why this is important

Solving a problem usually involves choosing from several possible solutions. Although your baby may not want to drop the toy at first, she will learn that it is not gone when she can no longer reach it. Her attempts at problem solving help her discover many solutions to finding the disappearing toy. This simple game serves as a model for solving more complex problems later in life.

What you do

● Cut a small hole in the top of a cardboard box and a larger hole low on the side of the box. Using one small object, show your child that it can be dropped through the hole in the top.

● Encourage her to look for the toy. *Can you see the toy? Where did it go?*

● Offer help if needed. If she tries to get the toy through the hole in the top, explain that the hole is too small for her hand and the toy is far away in the bottom of the box. If necessary, move the box slightly so she can see the toy through the side hole.

● Notice how she learns to look for the toy through the larger hole after playing the game several times. She may turn the box or crawl around it to find the larger hole.

● Limit the amount of help you offer each time you play. Give her a chance to drop the toy in and find it by herself.

Another idea

Add variety to the game by using different objects to drop in the box. Talk about the name of each object, along with the color or texture: *You're dropping the orange block!*

Let's read together!

One Duck Stuck
by Phillis Root and Jane Chapman

First Crayons

You made red marks on your paper!

Give your child a crayon and paper and talk about any marks he makes.

Playing with crayons and paper introduces your baby to using tools for drawing and writing. Your words let him know that this activity is important.

Why this is important

Crayons provide an easy introduction to writing tools. The simple act of putting a crayon to paper gives your baby a chance to freely explore some of the elements of drawing and writing. He will enjoy moving his arm and hand and seeing the result. Later he will learn to use crayons to express himself creatively.

What you do

● Tape a large piece of paper on the table. Seat your baby at the table and offer him one crayon. He may taste it, feel it, or show it to you. Talk about the crayon. *This is a red crayon. It is smooth and round.*

● Wait for him to make an accidental mark on the paper, or choose another crayon and make a small mark yourself.

● Offer positive encouragement when he makes a mark. *You made red lines with your crayon!* He may make long strokes or just poke at the paper.

● Give him a crayon only when he is seated in front of paper and can freely explore. **Do not leave your child alone with crayons or any other small objects that could be swallowed. Let him explore with crayons only while you are watching to make sure he uses them safely.**

Ready to move on?

When he has practiced with a crayon many times, offer him a choice between two crayons. Eventually, he will be able to choose a crayon from a variety placed before him.

Let's read together!

The Shape of Things
by Julie Lacome

Things to Taste

What's under the lid?

Describe your baby's experiences as she touches and tastes things.

Your baby may connect your words to what her senses are telling her as she explores.

Why this is important

Babies put everything in their mouths because tasting is one of the ways they find out about new objects. After they have tasted and handled something, they decide whether or not they like it. This activity encourages your baby to practice using all of her senses together. Letting her choose from among several tastes establishes positive attitudes toward new eating experiences and helps her learn to make choices.

What you do

- Sit with your baby where she usually eats her meals.

- Encourage her to taste things by putting a few items within easy reach. Try a slice of banana, a spoon, a peeled and very thin apple slice, or a cracker. **Be sure to give only things you are confident your child will not choke on. If you are unsure, save specific foods or this entire activity until your child is older.**

- Let her choose what she wants and let her taste as long as she wants. She may not eat the item, but simply use her mouth to explore. Talk about her choice. *The spoon is smooth and cool. That's a sweet apple!*

- Describe her actions as she makes choices. With each item, she may drop it and try something else immediately or she may show interest in only a single item. *You really like the banana.*

Ready to move on?

When you see that she enjoys looking under objects, try this. Sit at the table with a cupcake pan filled with items of different textures and smells, such as a spoonful of pureed vegetable, a bit of ice pop, or a slice of seedless orange. Lay a lid over each cup. Encourage her to lift the lids and try the contents. Observe and describe her experience with words such as *sweet*, *cold*, and *wet*.

Let's read together!

My Food Mi Comida
by Rebecca Emberley

Find a Picture

Look at that cat.

Name a picture and then turn it away from your baby so he can try to find it.

Using language to help your baby locate an item out of sight helps him remember the names of objects.

He's gone. Can you find the cat?

Why this is important

Naming a picture before making it disappear helps your child to associate the words with the picture. Using language is one way to help your child remember what he is looking for. Hearing the words will bring to mind the picture if he has seen it a few seconds before. As his memory develops, more time can pass between seeing and recalling.

What you do

- Attach a large picture of something familiar to your child, such as a teddy bear, baby, or cat, to a cardboard box.

- Sit with your baby on the floor. Show him the box with the picture attached. Talk about the picture: *Look, it is a picture of a baby. The baby is smiling.*

- Encourage your child to explore the picture. Then turn the box to move the picture out of his sight. *Where is the baby?* If he does not look for the picture, repeat the game from the beginning.

- Offer positive feedback for his efforts. *You moved the box to find the baby!* He might reach toward the box and flip it over or crawl around it to see the other side.

Ready to move on?

After playing several times with the same picture, add another picture to the second side of the box. Now ask the child to find first one picture and then the other. After two or more pictures have been added, he must make a choice. *Baby. Find the baby.*

Let's read together!

Where Is My Friend?
by Simms Taback

Making Useful Choices

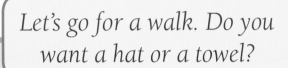

Let's go for a walk. Do you want a hat or a towel?

Let your baby choose between two things during an everyday task, one that is useful and one that is not.

Your baby will have a chance to make choices and learn from the results.

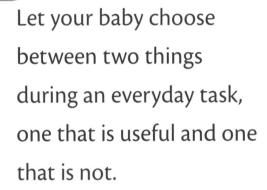

It's time to eat. Would you like a spoon or a lid?

Why this is important

Choosing between two objects on the basis of their usefulness is an early step in the process of learning how to evaluate. Adding a few safe choices to his day opens up new possibilities for him to have some control. Making these choices helps him to understand what an object can do and what is needed for a particular task. With practice he can choose the right tool for each job.

What you do

- Give your child two choices of objects to use when he needs to complete a task. For example, if he is ready to drink, let him choose between an empty cup and a full one. When he is ready to eat, offer him the choice of a spoon or a plastic lid. When it is time to wash hands, show him a block and a bar of soap. When it is time to take a walk, offer him a hat or a towel. Let him choose which item he wants.

- Let your child play with the item, even if he chooses the less useful option. Laugh with him as he enjoys the silliness of washing his hands with a block, for example.

- Show him the two choices again and give him a chance to choose more appropriately. *Do you want water? Which cup has the water?* At first, he may choose the less useful object, but with experience he will intentionally choose the more useful one.

Another idea

Add as many choices to his day as you can. Let him feel in control when there is no harm in either option. *Would you like to play with your truck or your fire engine?*

Let's read together!

Wibbly Pig Likes Bananas
by Mick Inkpen